My Little One

© Monique Hardman 2024

The rights of Monique Hardman to be identified as the author of this work have been asserted by her in accordance with the Copyright, Designs and Patents Act of 1988.

All rights reserved; no part of this publication may be reproduced, stored in a retrieval system, or transmitted in any form or by any means, electronic, mechanical, photocopying, recording or otherwise without the prior written consent of the publisher or a licence permitting copying in the UK issued by the Copyright Licensing Agency Ltd. www.cla.co.uk

ISBN 978-1-78792-046-0

Book design, layout and production management by Into Print
www.intoprint.net
+44 (0)1604 832149

MONIQUE HARDMAN

My Little One

Dedicated to my son,
Maverick.
Who fills my heart with endless joy,
and gave me life's greatest gift.
Who inspired me to pursue my passion.
I will love and guide you to
never let go of your dreams.

The smell of your hair,
your soft little feet.
The way you smile
and look up at me.
Your warm gentle hugs
and soft little tugs;
looking for comfort
before the days done.
And as much as you need me
you will never quite know,
I needed you more
in order to grow.

And through each stage,
I fall in love again.
And though it's bittersweet
as pieces of you change,
I get to see the parts of you
that will make a man one day.

Your long little lashes
tickling mine,
like butterfly kisses
she gave me at night.
And as I gently pet your arm,
to help you drift to sleep,
I remember the ways
she comforted me.
My mother is still here
lulling us to sleep.

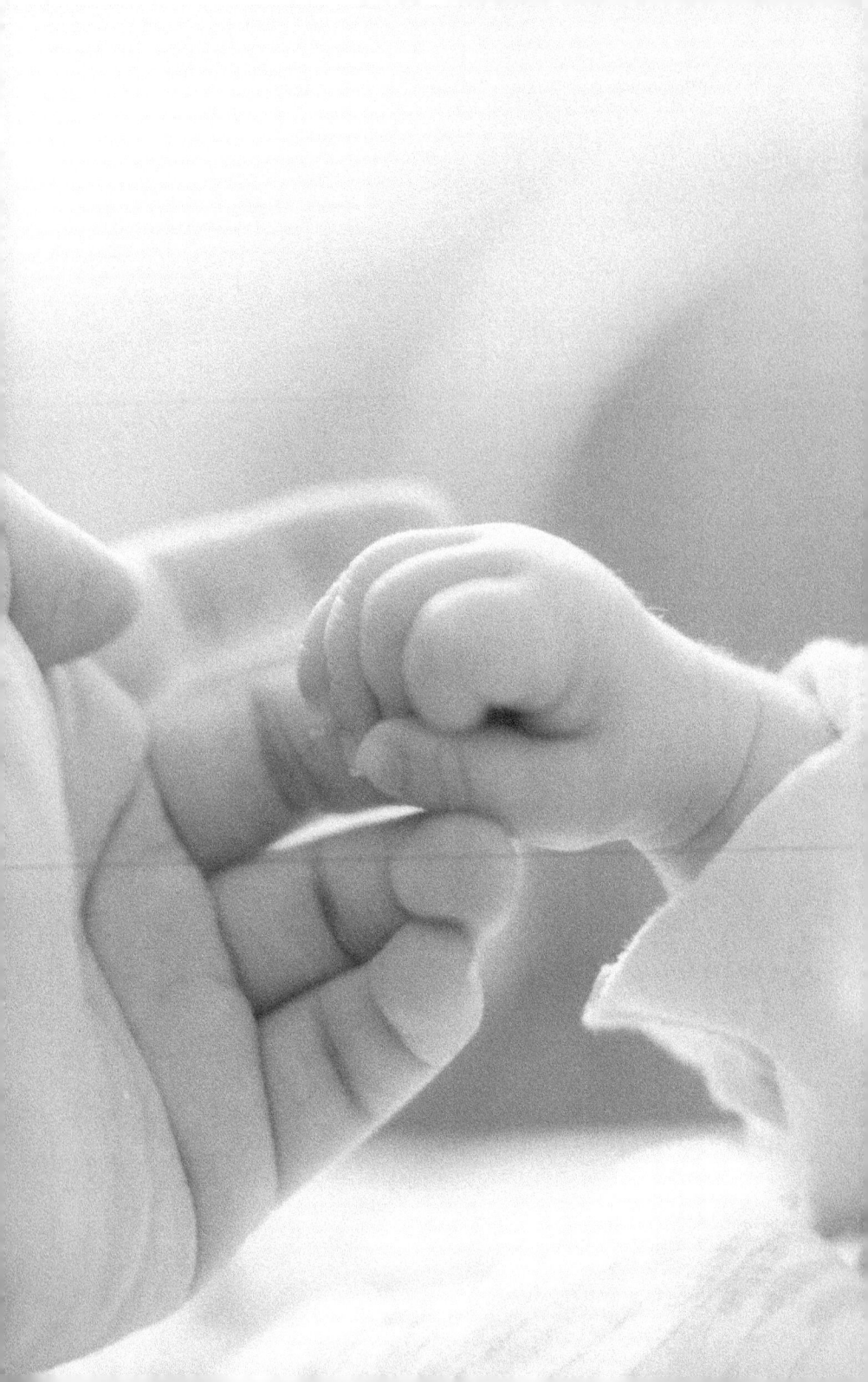

Who knew two little hands
could hold all my love,
and be filled with endless wonder.

You've been fed, clothed,
cuddled and loved,
but now it's time to drift off
to the skies above.
Where you will dream, grow,
and see magical things.
And when you wake
you will realize all
the possibilities.

I couldn't be more proud
of all you have endured.
Through every fall and setback,
you remain so pure.
And as I watch you sleep
I come to realize this,
that you and I are quite the same;
goodnight my little prince.

And sometimes I wonder
what dreams you will discover,
and how you will find love and joy.

It's time to drift to sleep,
lay your worries on me.
I'll be here to catch you,
while you dream.
Close your eyes,
I'll hold you tight
all throughout the night.
As you rest, float away
to a magical place.
And when you wake
I'll be here
to inspire,
love, and play.

How resilient
for such a little mind.
He falls and cries,
but then gets up another time.
As sweet and innocent he may seem,
he does not let fear take the lead.
He gets up again and must realize,
that one day he will stand
while learning to rise.

It's as if I'm seeing the world
for the first time through your eyes.
To feel life with an innocence, and hope
I had almost forgotten.
Remembering that the imaginable
is still possible
within all of us.

And like the sun you shine
when you are having fun,
but please slow down my little one.
Your eyes sparkle at the stars
with curiosity.
Slow down my little one.
The way you climb to reach the sky.
Slow down my little one.
Your voice echoes strongly between the trees.
Slow down my little one.
So bittersweet to see
your growth outside of me.
And as I let you wander
little by little;
my arms will always be here
to take in your warm embrace.

If we only gave ourselves
the same grace we show others.
The same excitement
we express for little ones;
one step at a time.

You almost forget,
what all that magic
and wonder feels like.
Then you watch that special movie,
that made you light up as a kid.
Remembering the imaginable is still possible,
within all of us.

As you drift to sleep,
I let go of the chaos from the day.
I find comfort in the rise and fall
of each breath you take.
My thoughts slow down,
my worries beat softly,
and my heart is at rest,
knowing we will awaken together
forever and always.

It's time to go nani,
it's time to go to sleep.
Lay your weary head on me
my bala jan,
jes sir'um em k'ez
my darling.

*English translation from Armenian:
nani- sleep
bala jan- "sweetheart"
jes sir'um em k'ez- I love you

And when the sun
kissed the sky,
yellow and blue
would fade to night.
Your star dancing in a stream,
as it lulled me back to sleep.

Knees scraped
and shoes filled with dirt;
your curious mind continues
when hurt.
You get up off your feet
and continue to run;
dancing and laughing
entrapped by the sun.

To watch you sleep
is a gift within itself.
I wonder where you go.
Do you float off to a magical place?
Are there hopes and dreams
you wish to face?
Or are you simply tucked in daddy's arms;
your favorite resting place.

I will love you,
guide you,
and walk beside you.
I will be there when you need,
but make sure you take the lead.
For this is how you learn to become
all that you can be.

Toes wrapped around my fingers,
little hands poking at my eyes.
Though the day has been long,
it is my favorite time.
To reconnect and love you
late into the night.
I'll take in every second;
won't let this moment
pass us by.

Like Christmas lights,
stars strung across the night sky.
Hoping the one burning brightest
is her heart lightening up,
for my little one to see.

www.ingramcontent.com/pod-product-compliance
Lightning Source LLC
Chambersburg PA
CBHW041929040426
42444CB00018B/3472